Save and Repair

Written by **DEBORAH CHANCELLOR**
Illustrated by **DIANE EWEN**

CRABTREE
PUBLISHING COMPANY
WWW.CRABTREEBOOKS.COM

Before, During, and After Reading Prompts

Activate Prior Knowledge and Make Predictions

Read the title of the book to the children and look at the illustrations. Ask children what they think the book may be about. Ask them questions related to the title, such as:

- Do you have a favorite toy? Where did you get it?
- What happens to your old toys, when you are finished playing with them?

During Reading

Stop at various points during reading and ask children questions related to the story:

- At first, what does Molly want to do with her toys? *(see pages 8–9)*
- What does Molly decide to do with her toy dinosaur, and why? *(pages 14–15)*
- Molly sorts her toys into three new piles. What is each pile for? How are these piles better for the environment? *(see pages 16–17)*
- What happens when Molly's friends come over to play? *(see pages 20–21)*
- Where do Mom and Molly take all the leftover toys? *(see pages 22–23)*

After Reading

Look at the information panels, then talk together about reusing toys. Ask children the following prompting questions:

- What is the problem with plastic toys? *(see page 9, 11)*
- What is most toy packaging made of, and what happens to it? *(see page 13)*
- How can you help reduce the number of new plastic toys that are made? *(see page 15)*
- What ways can we help reduce plastic waste that comes from toys? *(see page 23)*

Do the Quiz together *(see pages 28–29)*. Refer back to the information panels to find answers.

Crabtree Publishing Company

www.crabtreebooks.com   1-800-387-7650

Published in Canada
Crabtree Publishing
616 Welland Ave.
St. Catharines, Ontario
L2M 5V6

Published in the United States
Crabtree Publishing
PMB 59051
350 Fifth Avenue, 59th Floor
New York, New York 10118

PUBLISHED IN 2020 BY CRABTREE PUBLISHING COMPANY

All rights reserved. No part of this publication may be reproduced, stored in a retrieval system or be transmitted in any form or by any means, electronic, mechanical, photocopying, recording, or otherwise, without the prior written permission of Crabtree Publishing Company.

First published in 2019 by Wayland (an imprint of Hachette Children's Group, part of Hodder and Stoughton)
Copyright © Hodder and Stoughton, 2019

Author: Deborah Chancellor
Illustrator: Diane Ewen
Editorial Director: Kathy Middleton
Editors: Sarah Peutrill, Ellen Rodger
Designer: Cathryn Gilbert
Print and production coordinator: Katherine Berti

Printed in the U.S.A./122019/CG20191101

Library and Archives Canada Cataloguing in Publication

Title: Save and repair / written by Deborah Chancellor ; illustrated by Diane Ewen.
Other titles: Save and mend
Names: Chancellor, Deborah, author. | Ewen, Diane (Illustrator), illustrator.
Description: Series statement: Good to be green | Previously published under title: Save and mend. London: Wayland, 2019. | Includes index. | "A story about why it's important to reuse things".
Identifiers: Canadiana (print) 20190194367 |
    Canadiana (ebook) 20190194375 |
    ISBN 9780778772866 (hardcover) |
    ISBN 9780778772934 (softcover) |
    ISBN 9781427124739 (HTML)
Subjects: LCSH: Repairing—Environmental aspects—Juvenile literature. | LCSH: Toys—Repairing—Juvenile literature. | LCSH: Sustainable living—Juvenile literature. | LCSH: Environmentalism—Juvenile literature.
Classification: LCC TT151 .C53 2020 | DDC j688.7/20288—dc23

Library of Congress Cataloging-in-Publication Data

CIP available at the Library of Congress
LCCN: 2019043964

Save and Repair

A story about why it's important to reuse things.

"Your room
is a mess!"
said Mom.

4

Molly looked around her room.
She liked it the way it was, with
toys all over the place.

So Molly didn't clean her room.
It got messier and messier,
until one day Molly tripped
over a toy and hurt her knee.

"Maybe I should clean my room after all," she said.

Molly sorted her toys into two piles: one pile of toys to keep, and the other to throw away.

Mom looked at the pile of unwanted toys. "You can't throw all those away!" she said.

TOSS

KEEP

We don't keep our **plastic** toys for very long. The problem with that is plastic can take over 500 years to break down in a **landfill site**!

"If you don't want these toys,
someone else will," Mom said.
"Let's fix any broken toys, and
give away what you don't want."

Nine out of ten toys are made of plastic. They break more quickly than toys made from wood or metal, and they are often impossible to **recycle**.

"But aren't new toys always better?" Molly asked.
"Not for the **environment**," Mom replied.
"If children traded toys instead of buying new ones, fewer toys would have to be made in the first place. This would save **energy** and cut **pollution**."

It's not just toys that are hard to recycle. The plastic **packaging** they come in also ends up in landfill sites or in the sea.

Molly picked up a bright blue dinosaur.
"This used to be my favorite," she said.
"If I give it to my friend instead of
tossing it out, there'll be less plastic
at the landfill site," she said.
"Great idea!" said Mom.

A good way to cut down on the number of toys made in **factories** is to buy fewer new toys. Think carefully before you ask for a new one!

Transporting
materials

Making toys

Packaging toys

Transporting toys

So Molly sorted out her toys again. This time, she made three piles: one for toys to be fixed...

TO FIX

TO TRADE

one for toys to be traded...

and one for toys
to be given away.

TO GIVE
AWAY

At school, Molly talked to her friends.

"Let's help the environment," she said.

"Come to my house and bring some toys you don't want. We can fix them, trade them, or give them away. That means they won't end up in the garbage."

New toys are often wrapped in layers of plastic packaging. This protects the toys, but so much plastic is bad for the environment.

So the next day, Molly's friends came around to play. They brought a big pile of toys with them.

They fixed the broken toys, and traded some of the toys they no longer played with.

Everyone had exciting new things to play with!

They took the leftover toys to a
second-hand store. "Someone will
enjoy playing with them," said Mom.

Look after your toys and fix them if they break, so you can pass them on when you have finished with them. **Reusing** toys means less energy and materials are used because fewer new toys are being made, packaged, and delivered.

Mom helped Molly carry her toys up to her room. "Excellent job," said Mom. "You didn't buy anything new or throw anything away!"

"That's cool!" said Molly.
"But where am I going
to put my new things?"

Mom rolled her eyes.
"Your room is a mess!"
she said.

But Molly didn't reply.
She was too busy
playing.

Quiz time

Which of these things are true? Read the book again to find out!

(Cover up the answers on page 29.)

1. Plastic toys take 100 years to break down when you throw them away.

2. Half of all toys are made of plastic.

3. Toys are easy to recycle.

4. Most toy packaging can be recycled.

5. You can reduce the number of toys being made by buying fewer new things.

Answers

1. **False**  A plastic toy at a landfill site can take over 500 years to break down. *(See pages 8–9)*

2. **False**  Nine out of ten toys—more than half—are made of plastic. *(See pages 10–11)*

3. **False**  Most toys are made of plastic, a material that is often impossible to recycle. *(See pages 10–11)*

4. **False**  Most toy packaging is made of plastic that can't be recycled. It ends up at landfill sites or in the ocean. *(See pages 12–13)*

5. **True**  Reusing a toy saves the energy and materials needed to make a new one. *(See pages 22–23)*

Get active

In this story, Molly and her friends get together to fix and trade their toys. Do the same thing at home with your friends. Ask your teacher if you can have a toy trading party at your school.

Hold a toy sale and invite your friends and family. After the sale, give the money you make to an environmental charity, such as WWF (World Wildlife Fund).

See for yourself how slowly plastic breaks down. Dig two holes in the ground and bury a plastic spoon in one hole and a wooden spoon in the other. Put a marker where you have buried the spoons, then dig them up three months later. What has happened to each of them?

Write a story about a toy that is saved from the garbage and sold at a second-hand store. Give your story a happy ending!

A note about sharing this book

The *Good to Be Green* series provides a starting point for further discussion on important environmental issues, such as pollution, climate change, and endangered wildlife. Each topic is relevant to both children and adults.

Save and Repair!

This story explores the issues of recycling and reusing in the toy industry. *Save and Repair!* contains practical suggestions for how to reuse toys, such as by fixing, trading, sharing, and selling them. The story also covers the wider issue of plastic waste. The story and the nonfiction elements in *Save and Repair!* encourage the reader to conclude that we should look after toys, so we can share them with others and reduce the need to use energy to make new toys.

How to use the book

Adults can share this book with individuals or groups of children, and use it as a starting point for discussion. Illustrations provide visual support for children who are starting to read on their own. Repetition is also used to reinforce understanding. For example the phrase "Your room's a mess!" is found at the beginning and end of the book, building familiarity and adding humor.

The story introduces vocabulary relevant to the theme of reusing, such as: *second-hand, energy, environment, factories, landfill, materials, packaging, plastic, pollution, recycle, repairing, reusing,* and *traded*. Unfamiliar vocabulary is in bold text, and defined in the glossary on page 32. When reading the story for the first time, refer to the glossary with the children.

There is also an index on page 32. Encourage children to use the index when you are talking about the book. For example, ask them to use the index to find the page that shows a second-hand store (page 22). It is important that children know that information can be found in books as well as searched for on the Internet with a responsible adult.

Glossary

energy Power that is used to make something work, such as electricity

environment The world around us

factories Buildings where things are made to be sold to people

landfill site A place where garbage is buried in the ground

materials What things are made of

packaging What something is wrapped in to protect it from damage

plastic A human-made material that can be molded into any shape

pollution Harmful chemicals or garbage that make the air or a place dirty

recycle Change something used into something useful

reusing To use something again and again. Toys can be reused by trading them with friends or giving them to be sold in second-hand stores.

second-hand store A store that sells used things

Index

energy 12, 23
environment 12, 18–19
factories 15
fix/repair 10, 16, 18, 21, 23

landfill site 9, 13
materials 15, 23
metal 11
packaging 13, 15, 19, 23

plastic 9, 11, 13–14, 19
pollution 12
recycle 11, 13
reuse 23
sea 13

second-hand store 22
trade 12, 16, 18, 21
wood 11